The Gift of Love

The Gift of Love

ZondervanPublishingHouse

A Division of HarperCollins*Publishers*

The Gift of Love
New International Version
Copyright ©1994
by The Zondervan Corporation
ISBN 0-310-96304-4
All Scripture quotations are taken from the HOLY BIBLE:
NEW INTERNATIONAL VERSION® (North American Edition). Copyright
©1973, 1978, 1984, by International Bible Society.
Used by permission of Zondervan Publishing House.
"NIV" and "New International Version" are registered in the United States Patent
and Trademark Office by International Bible Society.

Project Editor: Leslie Berg Hoffman
Design: Jody Langley
Illustration: Judy L. Miller
Printed in Hong Kong
94 95 96 / HK / 3 2 1

To:_____

Treasure these gifts of love
from the Bible.

From:_____

Gifts of God's Love

Know therefore that
the LORD your God is God;
he is the faithful God,
keeping his covenant of love
to a thousand generations
of those who love him and
keep his commands.

Deuteronomy 7:9

O LORD, God of Israel,
there is no God like you
in heaven or on earth – you who
keep your covenant of love
with your servants who continue
wholeheartedly in your way.

2 Chronicles 6:14

But I trust
in your unfailing love;
my heart rejoices in
your salvation.
Psalm 13:5

Surely goodness and love
will follow me all the days of my life,
and I will dwell in the house
of the LORD forever.

Psalm 23:6

Your love, O LORD,
reaches to the heavens,
your faithfulness to the skies.
Psalm 36:5

How priceless is
your unfailing love!
Both high and low among men
find refuge in the shadow of
your wings.
Psalm 36:7

By day the LORD directs his love,
at night his song is with me –
a prayer to the God of my life.

Psalm 42:8

But I will sing of your strength,
in the morning I will sing of your love;
for you are my fortress,
my refuge in times of trouble.

Psalm 59:16

You are forgiving and good,
O Lord, abounding in love to all
who call to you.
Psalm 86:5

For great is your love toward me;
you have delivered me from the
depths of the grave.

Psalm 86:13

From everlasting to
everlasting the LORD's love
is with those who fear him,
and his righteousness with
their children's children.

Psalm 103:17

The Lord is gracious
and compassionate,
slow to anger
and rich in love.

Psalm 145:8

The Lord appeared
to us in the past, saying:
"I have loved you
with an everlasting love;
I have drawn you
with loving-kindness."

Jeremiah 31:3

The LORD your God is with you,
he is mighty to save.
He will take great delight in you,
he will quiet you with his love,
he will rejoice over you with singing.

Zephaniah 3:17

For God so loved the world
that he gave his one and only Son,
that whoever believes in him
shall not perish but have eternal life.

John 3:16

If anyone loves me,
he will obey my teaching.
My Father will love him,
and we will come to him and
make our home with him.

John 14:23

As the Father has loved me,
so have I loved you.
Now remain in my love.
If you obey my commands,
you will remain in my love,
just as I have obeyed my Father's
commands and remain in his love.

John 15:9-10

God has poured out his love
into our hearts by the Holy Spirit,
whom he has given us.
Romans 5:5

But God demonstrates
his own love for us in this:
While we were still sinners,
Christ died for us.

Romans 5:8

Aim for perfection,
listen to my appeal,
be of one mind, live in peace.
And the God of love
and peace will be with you.
2 Corinthians 13:11

In love he predestined us
to be adopted as his sons through
Jesus Christ, in accordance
with his pleasure and will – to
the praise of his glorious grace,
which he has freely given us
in the One he loves.

Ephesians 1:4-6

Because of his great love for us,
God, who is rich in mercy,
made us alive with Christ
even when we were dead in
transgressions – it is by grace
you have been saved.
Ephesians 2:4-5

May our Lord Jesus Christ
himself and God our Father,
who loved us and by his grace
gave us eternal encouragement
and good hope, encourage
your hearts and strengthen you
in every good deed and word.

2 Thessalonians 2:16-17

But when the kindness and
love of God our Savior appeared,
he saved us, not because
of righteous things we had done,
but because of his mercy.

Titus 3:4-5

If anyone obeys his word,
God's love is truly
made complete in him.
1 John 2:5

How great is the love
the Father has lavished on us,
that we should be called
children of God!
1 John 3:1

This is how God
showed his love among us:
He sent his one and only Son
into the world that we might
live through him.
1 John 4:9

God is love.
Whoever lives in love lives in God,
and God in him. In this way,
love is made complete among us
so that we will have confidence
on the day of judgment, because
in this world we are like him.

1 John 4:16-17

There is no fear in love.
But perfect love drives out fear,
because fear has to do with
punishment. The one who fears
is not made perfect in love.

1 John 4:18

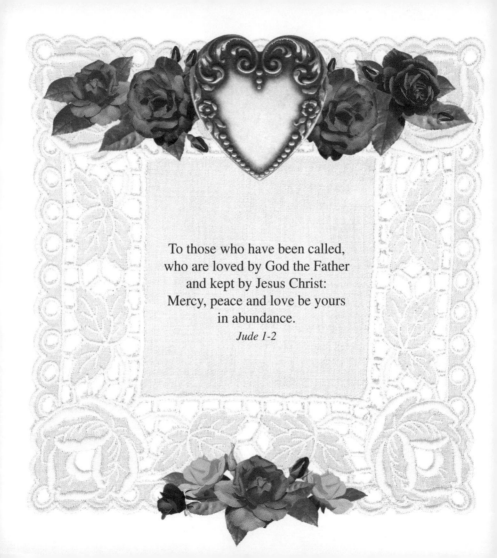

To those who have been called,
who are loved by God the Father
and kept by Jesus Christ:
Mercy, peace and love be yours
in abundance.

Jude 1-2

Gifts
of
Christ's
Love

My command is this:
Love each other as I have loved you.
Greater love has no one than this,
that he lay down his life for
his friends. You are my friends if
you do what I command.

John 15:12-14

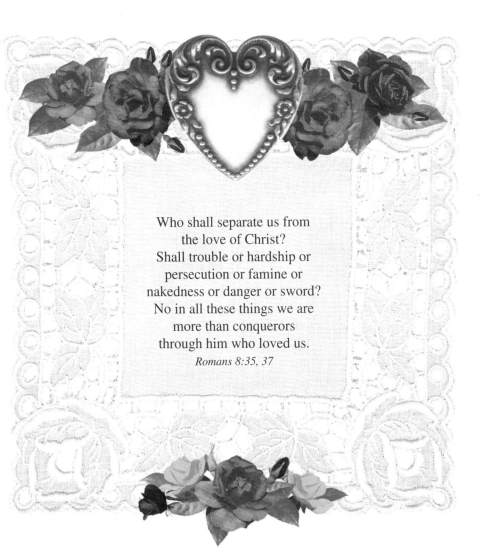

Who shall separate us from
the love of Christ?
Shall trouble or hardship or
persecution or famine or
nakedness or danger or sword?
No in all these things we are
more than conquerors
through him who loved us.

Romans 8:35, 37

I pray that you,
being rooted and established
in love, may have power,
together with all the saints,
to grasp how wide and long and
high and deep is the love of Christ,
and to know this love that
surpasses knowledge.

Ephesians 3:17-19

Husbands, love your wives,
just as Christ loved the church
and gave himself up for her.
Ephesians 5:25

Those whom I love
I rebuke and discipline.
So be earnest, and repent.
Revelation 3:19

Gifts of Love for God

Love the LORD your God
with all your heart and
with all your soul and with
all your strength.

Deuteronomy 6:5

Love the LORD, all his saints!
The LORD preserves the faithful,
but the proud he pays back in full.
Psalm 31:23

"Because he loves me,"
says the LORD,
"I will rescue him; I will
protect him, for he
acknowledges my name."
Psalm 91:14

And we know that
in all things God works for the
good of those who love him,
who have been called according
to his purpose.

Romans 8:28

As it is written:
"No eye has seen, no ear
has heard, no mind has conceived
what God has prepared for
those who love him."

1 Corinthians 2:9

Blessed is the man
who perseveres under trial,
because when he has stood the test,
he will receive the crown of life
that God has promised to
those who love him.
James 1:12

We love because he first loved us.
If anyone says, "I love God,"
yet hates his brother, he is a liar.
For anyone who does not love
his brother, whom he has seen,
cannot love God,
whom he has not seen.

1 John 4:19-20

And he has given us
this command:
Whoever loves God
must also love his brother.
1 John 4:21

This is love for God:
to obey his commands.
1 John 5:3

Gifts of Love for Christ

Anyone who loves his
father or mother more than me
is not worthy of me;
anyone who loves his son or
daughter more than me
is not worthy of me.

Matthew 10:37

Jesus said to them,
"If God were your Father,
you would love me, for I came
from God and now am here.
I have not come on my own;
but he sent me."

John 8:42

If anyone loves me,
he will obey my teaching.
My Father will love him,
and we will come to him and
make our home with him.
John 14:23

He who does not love me
will not obey my teaching.
These words you hear
are not my own; they belong
to the Father who sent me.
John 14:24

Grace to all who love
our Lord Jesus Christ with
an undying love.
Ephesians 6:24

Gifts
of Love
for
Others

You have heard that it was said,
"Love your neighbor
and hate your enemy."
But I tell you:
Love your enemies and pray
for those who persecute you.
Matthew 5:43-44

A new command I give you:
Love one another.
As I have loved you,
so you must love one another.
By this all men will know that
you are my disciples,
if you love one another.

John 13:34-35

Love must be sincere.
Hate what is evil;
cling to what is good.
Be devoted to one another
in brotherly love.
Honor one another
above yourselves.
Romans 12:9-10

Let no debt remain outstanding,
except the continuing debt
to love one another,
for he who loves his fellowman
has fulfilled the law...
"Love your neighbor as yourself."

Romans 13:8, 9

Love is patient, love is kind.
It does not envy, it does not boast,
it is not proud. It is not rude,
it is not self-seeking,
it is not easily angered,
it keeps no record of wrongs.
1 Corinthians 13:4-5

Love does not delight in evil
but rejoices with the truth.
It always protects, always trusts,
always hopes, always perseveres.
Love never fails.
1 Corinthians 13:6-8

And now these three remain:
faith, hope and love.
But the greatest of these is love.
1 Corinthians 13:13

Do everything in love.
1 Corinthians 16:14

Be completely humble and
gentle; be patient, bearing with
one another in love.
Ephesians 4:2

Now that you have purified
yourselves by obeying the truth
so that you have sincere love
for your brothers, love one
another deeply, from the heart.
1 Peter 1:22

Live in harmony with one another;
be sympathetic, love as brothers,
be compassionate and humble.
1 Peter 3:8

This is how we know what love is:
Jesus Christ laid down his life for us.
And we ought to lay down our
lives for our brothers.

1 John 3:16

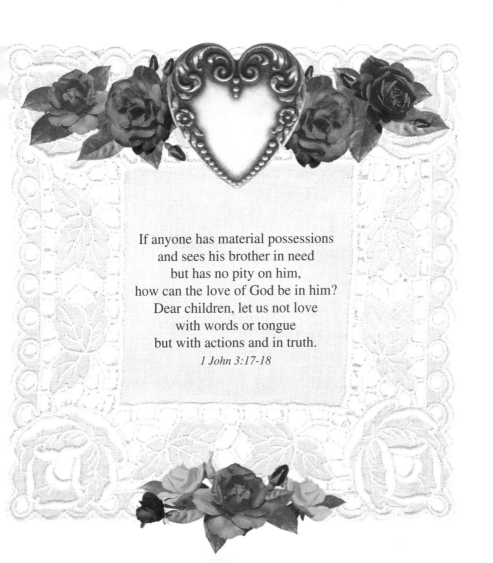

If anyone has material possessions
and sees his brother in need
but has no pity on him,
how can the love of God be in him?
Dear children, let us not love
with words or tongue
but with actions and in truth.

1 John 3:17-18

Dear friends,
since God so loved us,
we also ought to love one another.
No one has ever seen God;
but if we love one another,
God lives in us and his love is
made complete in us.

1 John 4:11-12

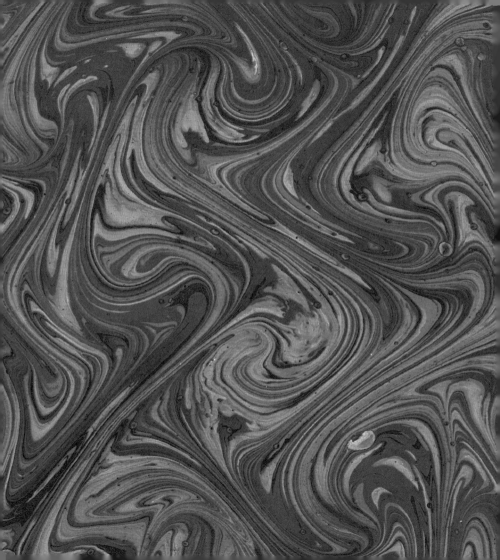